MIT LUFTPOST
PAR AVION

This journal belongs to

_____

TRAVEL

© 2008 Ellie Claire Gift & Paper Corp.

www.ellieclaire.com

Designed by Lisa and Jeff Franke, Lemon Lulu Studios, Minneapolis, MN

Scripture references are from the following sources: The Holy Bible, New International Version® NIV®.
© 1973, 1978, 1984 by International Bible Society. Used by permission of Zondervan. The NEW AMERICAN
STANDARD BIBLE® (NASB), © Copyright The Lockman Foundation 1960, 1962, 1963, 1968, 1971, 1972,
1973, 1975, 1977, 1995. Used by permission. (www.Lockman.org). The New King James Version (NKJV).
Copyright © 1982 by Thomas Nelson, Inc. Used by permission. The New Century Version® (NCV).
Copyright © 1987, 1988, 1991 by Thomas Nelson, Inc. Used by permission. The Message © 1993, 1994,
1995, 1996, 2000, 2001, 2002 by Eugene Peterson. Used by permission of NavPress, Colorado Springs, CO.
The Holy Bible, New Living Translation® (NLT). Copyright © 1996, 2004. Used by permission of
Tyndale House Publishers, Inc., www.newlivingtranslation.com. All rights reserved.

ISBN 978-1-934770-31-3

Printed in China

Cⁱᵉ GÉNÉRALE TRANSATLANTIQUE

For the Lord your God will be
with you wherever you go.

JOSHUA 1:9

560

Imp. A. François, Paris   Modèle 137

Ellie
Elaire
gift & paper expressions

...inspired by life

THOUGHT FOR THE DAY

They say you will never be lonely from the start of each day to its end
if you walk life's pathway with love in your heart, and side by side with a friend.

HIGHLIGHT OF THE DAY

*W*alk in the paths He shows you: follow the life-map absolutely,
keep an eye out for the signposts...then you'll get on well in
whatever you do and wherever you go.

1 KINGS 2:1 THE MESSAGE

Don't hurry, don't worry. You're only here for a short visit
so be sure to smell the flowers along the way.

Walter Hagen

HIGHLIGHT OF THE DAY

....

....

....

....

....

....

....

....

*Steep your life in God-reality, God-initiative, God-provisions.
Don't worry about missing out. You'll find all your everyday
human concerns will be met.*

MATTHEW 6:33 THE MESSAGE

THOUGHT FOR THE DAY

Though we travel the world over to find the beautiful,
we must carry it with us or we find it not.

Ralph Waldo Emerson

HIGHLIGHT OF THE DAY

....
....
....
....
....
....
....
....
....

I run in the path of Your commands,
for You have set my heart free.
PSALM 119:32 NIV

THOUGHT FOR THE DAY

Do not follow where the path may lead.
Go instead where there is no path and leave a trail.

T. S. Eliot

HIGHLIGHT OF THE DAY

I am guiding you in the way of wisdom,
and I am leading you on the right path.
PROVERBS 4:11 NCV

THOUGHT FOR THE DAY

For my part, I travel not to go anywhere, but to go. I travel for travel's sake.

Robert Louis Stevenson

24,349

HIGHLIGHT OF THE DAY

*Y*our life is a journey you must travel
with a deep consciousness of God.
1 PETER 1:18 THE MESSAGE

THOUGHT FOR THE DAY

I have wandered all my life, and I have traveled; the difference between the
two is this—we wander for distraction, but we travel for fulfillment.

Hilaire Belloc

HIGHLIGHT OF THE DAY

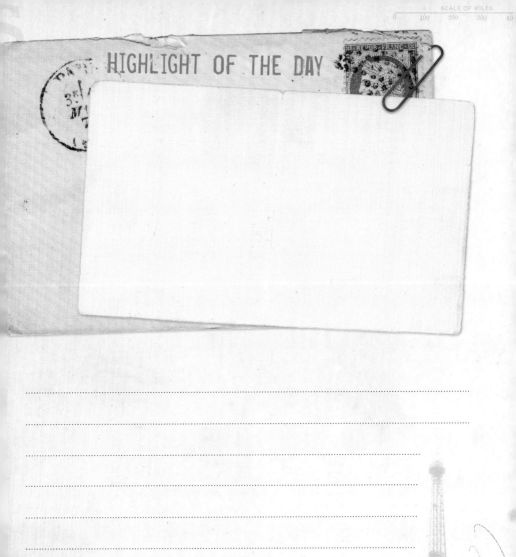

*Y*ou see me when I travel and when I rest at home.
You know everything I do.
PSALM 139:3 NLT

THOUGHT FOR THE DAY

Adventure is worthwhile in itself.

Amelia Earhart

Your word is like a lamp for my feet
and a light for my path.
PSALM 119:105 NCV

THOUGHT FOR THE DAY

There is no pleasure in having nothing to do;
the fun is in having lots to do and not doing it.

Mary Wilson Little

What I'm trying to do here is to get you to relax, to not be so preoccupied with *getting*, so you can respond to God's *giving*.

MATTHEW 6:32 THE MESSAGE

THOUGHT FOR THE DAY

Savor little glimpses of God's goodness and His majesty, thankful for the gift
of them: winding pathways through the woods, a bright green canopy overhead,
and dappled sunshine falling all around.

HIGHLIGHT OF THE DAY

*H*onor and majesty are before Him;
strength and beauty are in His sanctuary.

PSALM 96:6 NKJV

THOUGHT FOR THE DAY

Walk on a rainbow trail; walk on a trail of song, and all about you will be beauty.
There is a way out of every dark mist, over a rainbow trail.

Navajo song

HIGHLIGHT OF THE DAY

I set My rainbow in the cloud, and it shall be for the sign
of the covenant between Me and the earth.

GENESIS 9:13 NKJV

THOUGHT FOR THE DAY

God will not send us out on any journey for which He does not equip us well.

Alexander Maclaren

24,349

HIGHLIGHT OF THE DAY

My God shall supply all your need according to
His riches in glory by Christ Jesus.
PHILIPPIANS 4:19 NKJV

In order to see where we are going, we not only must remember where
we have been, but we must understand where we have been.

Ella Baker

HIGHLIGHT OF THE DAY

Wisdom begins with respect for the Lord; those who obey His orders have good understanding. He should be praised forever.

PSALM 111:10 NCV

THOUGHT FOR THE DAY

Two roads diverged in a wood, and I—I took the one less traveled by, and that has made all the difference.

Robert Frost

HIGHLIGHT OF THE DAY

You shall walk in all the ways which the Lord
your God has commanded you, that you
may live and that it may be well with you.

DEUTERONOMY 5:33 NKJV

THOUGHT FOR THE DAY

Our days are identical suitcases—all the same size—
but some people can pack more into them than others.

Bits & Pieces

HIGHLIGHT OF THE DAY

*T*each us to number our days aright,
that we may gain a heart of wisdom.
PSALM 90:12 NIV

THOUGHT FOR THE DAY
Friendship brings people close no matter
how great the distance between them.

HIGHLIGHT OF THE DAY

The amazing grace of the Master, Jesus Christ, the extravagant love of God, the intimate friendship of the Holy Spirit, be with all of you.

2 CORINTHIANS 13:14 THE MESSAGE

THOUGHT FOR THE DAY

He who does not get fun and enjoyment out of everyday
needs to reorganize his life.

George M. Adams

HIGHLIGHT OF THE DAY

The steps of a good man are ordered by the Lord,
and he delights in His way.
PSALM 37:23 NKJV

THOUGHT FOR THE DAY

Around me when I look, His handiwork I see;
This world is like a picture book to teach His love to me.

Jane E. Leeson

HIGHLIGHT OF THE DAY

For since the creation of the world God's invisible qualities—
His eternal power and divine nature—have been clearly seen.

ROMANS 1:20 NIV

THOUGHT FOR THE DAY

Security is mostly a superstition. It does not exist in nature....
Life is either a daring adventure or nothing.

Helen Keller

HIGHLIGHT OF THE DAY

God, who got you started in this spiritual adventure, shares
with us the life of His Son and our Master Jesus.
1 CORINTHIANS 1:7 THE MESSAGE

THOUGHT FOR THE DAY

God give me joy in the tasks that press, in the memories that burn and bless;
In the thought that life has love to spend, in the faith that God's at journey's end.

Thomas Curtis Clark

Work hard and serve the Lord enthusiastically. Rejoice in our
confident hope. Be patient in trouble, and keep on praying....
Always be eager to practice hospitality.

ROMANS 12:11-13 NLT

Remember, no matter where you go, there you are.

Earl Mac Rauch

HIGHLIGHT OF THE DAY

I am with you and will watch over you wherever you go....
I will not leave you until I have done what I have promised you.

GENESIS 28:15 NIV

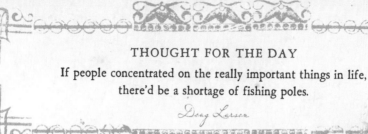

THOUGHT FOR THE DAY

If people concentrated on the really important things in life,
there'd be a shortage of fishing poles.

Doug Larson

HIGHLIGHT OF THE DAY

Is not life more important than food [and] clothes? Look at the
birds of the air; they do not sow or reap..., and yet your heavenly
Father feeds them. Are you not much more valuable than they?

MATTHEW 6:25-26 NIV

THOUGHT FOR THE DAY

To travel hopefully is a better thing than to arrive.

Robert Louis Stevenson

HIGHLIGHT OF THE DAY

....

....

....

....

....

....

....

....

*He protected us on our entire journey and among
all the nations through which we traveled.*

JOSHUA 24:17 NIV

THOUGHT FOR THE DAY

The longer I live, the more my mind dwells upon the
beauty and the wonder of the world.

John Burroughs

HIGHLIGHT OF THE DAY

....
....
....
....
....
....
....
....

*M*ake God's glory resound; echo His praises
from coast to coast.
ISAIAH 42:10 THE MESSAGE

Like all great travelers, I have seen more than I remember,
and remember more than I have seen.

Benjamin Disraeli

Light is sweet, and it pleases the eyes to see the sun. However many years a man may live, let him enjoy them all.
ECCLESIASTES 11:7-8 NIV

THOUGHT FOR THE DAY

There will stretch out before you an ever-lengthening, ever-ascending, ever-improving path.... But this, far from discouraging, only adds to the joy and glory of the climb.

Sir Winston Churchill

HIGHLIGHT OF THE DAY

So we have been greatly encouraged in the midst of
our troubles and suffering, dear brothers and sisters,
because you have remained strong in your faith.

1 THESSALONIANS 3:7 NLT

THOUGHT FOR THE DAY

Little acts of kindness which we render to each other in everyday life,
are like flowers by the way-side to the traveler: they serve to gladden
the heart and relieve the tedium of life's journey.

Eunice Bathrick

HIGHLIGHT OF THE DAY

If your gift is to encourage others, be encouraging.
If it is giving, give generously.... And if you have a
gift for showing kindness to others, do it gladly.

ROMANS 12:8 NLT

THOUGHT FOR THE DAY

Nature has been for me, for as long as I can remember,
a source of solace, inspiration, adventure, and delight.

Lorraine Anderson

HIGHLIGHT OF THE DAY

God's Word and our prayers make every item in creation holy.
1 TIMOTHY 4:1 THE MESSAGE

THOUGHT FOR THE DAY

A new path lies before us; we're not sure where it leads;
but God goes on before us, providing all our needs.

Linda Maurice

HIGHLIGHT OF THE DAY

Trust in the Lord with all your heart, and lean not on your own understanding; In all your ways acknowledge Him, and He shall direct your paths.

PROVERBS 3:5-6 NKJV

THOUGHT FOR THE DAY

You have to allow a certain amount of time in which you are doing nothing
in order to have things occur to you, to let your mind think.

Mortimer J. Alder

HIGHLIGHT OF THE DAY

Whatever is true, whatever is noble, whatever is right, whatever
is pure, whatever is lovely, whatever is admirable—if anything
is excellent or praiseworthy—think about such things.

PHILIPPIANS 4:8 NIV

THOUGHT FOR THE DAY

At every crossroad, follow your dream. It is courageous
to let your heart lead the way.

Thomas Leland

My aim is to raise hopes by pointing the way to life
without end. This is the life God promised
long ago—and He doesn't break promises!

TITUS 1:1 THE MESSAGE

May your life become one of glad and unending praise to the Lord as you
journey through this world, and in the world that is to come!

Teresa of Avila

....

....

....

....

....

....

....

....

....

....

....

....

....

....

....

HIGHLIGHT OF THE DAY

All praise to God, the Father of our Lord Jesus Christ,
who has blessed us with every spiritual blessing in the
heavenly realms because we are united with Christ.

EPHESIANS 1:3 NLT

THOUGHT FOR THE DAY

When preparing to travel, lay out all your clothes and all your money.
Then take half the clothes and twice the money.

Susan Heller

HIGHLIGHT OF THE DAY

*You gave me life and showed me kindness, and in your
providence watched over my spirit.*

JOB 10:12 NIV

THOUGHT FOR THE DAY

Only those who will risk going too far can possibly
find out how far one can go.

T. S. Eliot

HIGHLIGHT OF THE DAY

To those who use well what they are given, even more will be given, and they will have an abundance.

MATTHEW 25:29 NLT

THOUGHT FOR THE DAY

Take a chance! All life is a chance. The man who goes furthest
is generally the one who is willing to do and dare.

Dale Carnegie

HIGHLIGHT OF THE DAY

Use every chance you have for doing good.

EPHESIANS 5:16 NCV

THOUGHT FOR THE DAY

Life...gives you the chance to love and to work
and to play and to look up at the stars.

Henry Van Dyke

HIGHLIGHT OF THE DAY

The heavens declare the glory of God, and the skies announce
what his hands have made. Day after day they tell the story;
night after night they tell it again.

PSALM 19:1-2 NCV

THOUGHT FOR THE DAY

God wanted to join us on the road, to listen to our story, and to help us realize that we are not walking in circles but moving toward the house of peace and joy.

Henri J. M. Nouwen

HIGHLIGHT OF THE DAY

I come back to my father's house in peace,
then the Lord shall be my God.

GENESIS 28:21 NKJV

THOUGHT FOR THE DAY
Think of whatever you are doing as an adventure
and watch your life change for the better.

Wilferd A. Peterson

HIGHLIGHT OF THE DAY

*E*mbracing what God does for you is the best thing
you can do for Him.... Fix your attention on God.
You'll be changed from the inside out.

ROMANS 12:1-2 THE MESSAGE

THOUGHT FOR THE DAY

One cannot collect all the beautiful shells on the beach. One can collect
only a few, and they are more beautiful if they are few.

Anne Morrow Lindbergh

HIGHLIGHT OF THE DAY

How precious to me are Your thoughts, O God!
How vast is the sum of them! Were I to count them,
they would outnumber the grains of sand.

PSALM 139:17-18 NIV

THOUGHT FOR THE DAY

When I look back at where I've been, I see that what I am becoming
is a whole lot further down the road from where I was.

Gloria Gaither

God is gently calling you...to an open place of freedom
where He has set your table full of the best food.

JOB 36:16 NCV

THOUGHT FOR THE DAY

Today is your day! Your mountain is waiting. So...get on your way.

Theodor Seuss Geisel (Dr. Seuss)

HIGHLIGHT OF THE DAY

Come, let us go up to the mountain of the Lord.... There He will teach us His ways, and we will walk in His paths.

ISAIAH 2:3 NLT

THOUGHT FOR THE DAY

May the God of love and peace set your heart at rest
and speed you on your journey.

Raymond of Penafort

HIGHLIGHT OF THE DAY

Love and truth belong to God's people;
goodness and peace will be theirs.

PSALM 85:10 NCV

THOUGHT FOR THE DAY

Discoveries are often made by...going off the main road,
by trying the untried.

Frank Tyger

HIGHLIGHT OF THE DAY

$\mathcal{D}$ear friend, listen well to my words.... Learn it by heart!
Those who discover these words live, really live;
body and soul, they're bursting with health.

PROVERBS 4:20-22 THE MESSAGE

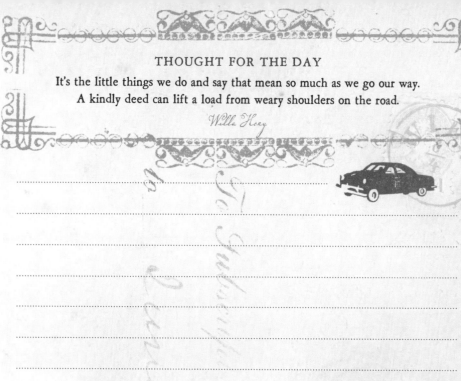

THOUGHT FOR THE DAY

It's the little things we do and say that mean so much as we go our way.
A kindly deed can lift a load from weary shoulders on the road.

Willa Hoey

*These things I have spoken to you so that My joy may
be in you, and that your joy may be made full.*

JOHN 15:11 NASB

THOUGHT FOR THE DAY

The most important trip you may take in life is meeting people halfway.

Henry Boye

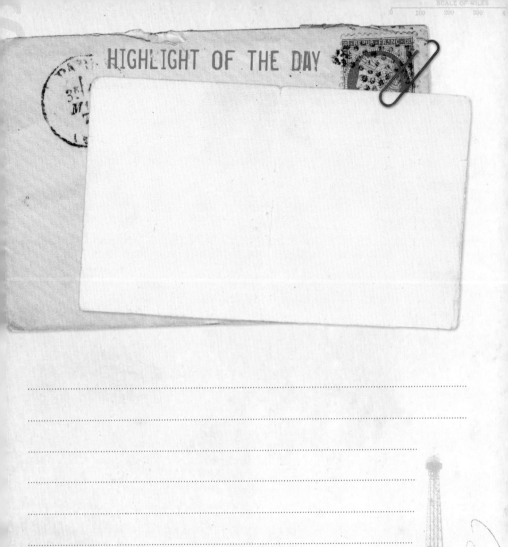

HIGHLIGHT OF THE DAY

Be joyful. Grow to maturity. Encourage each other. Live in harmony and peace. Then the God of love and peace will be with you.

2 CORINTHIANS 13:11 NLT

THOUGHT FOR THE DAY

Every now and then go away, have a little relaxation. For when you
come back to your work, your judgment will be surer.

Leonardo da Vinci

HIGHLIGHT OF THE DAY

The instructions of the Lord are perfect,
reviving the soul.
PSALM 19:7 NLT

*G*od, your God, carried you as
a father carries his child.

DEUTERONOMY 1:29 THE MESSAGE

THOUGHT FOR THE DAY

What we call the end is also a beginning. The end is where we start from.

T. S. Eliot

24,349

HIGHLIGHT OF THE DAY

He has planted eternity in the human heart,
but even so, people cannot see the
whole scope of God's work from beginning to end.
ECCLESIASTES 3:11 NLT

THOUGHT FOR THE DAY

If we never met again in our lives I should feel that somehow the whole adventure of existence was justified by my having met you.

Lewis Mumford

HIGHLIGHT OF THE DAY

My dear brothers and sisters, stay true to the Lord. I love you
and long to see you, dear friends, for you are my joy
and the crown I receive for my work.

PHILIPPIANS 4:1 NLT

THOUGHT FOR THE DAY

Certainly, travel is more than the seeing of sights; it is a change that goes on, deep and permanent, in the ideas of living.

Miriam Beard

24,349

HIGHLIGHT OF THE DAY

The right time has come. The kingdom of God is near.
Change your hearts and lives and believe the Good News!
MARK 1:15 NCV

THOUGHT FOR THE DAY

May the road rise to meet you, may the wind be always at your back...
And, until we meet again, may God hold you in the palm of His hand.

Irish Blessing

HIGHLIGHT OF THE DAY

𝒯he Lord bless you, and keep you; The Lord make
His face shine on you, And be gracious to you.

NUMBERS 6:24-25 NASB

THOUGHT FOR THE DAY

The really happy person is one who can enjoy
the scenery on a detour.

The signposts of God are clear and point out the right road.
The life-maps of God are right, showing the way to joy.

PSALM 19:7-8 THE MESSAGE

THOUGHT FOR THE DAY

In the long run, the pessimist may be proved to be right,
but the optimist has a better time on the trip.

Daniel L. Reardon

HIGHLIGHT OF THE DAY

Put your hope in the Lord.
Travel steadily along His path.
PSALM 37:34 NLT

24,349

HIGHLIGHT OF THE DAY

....
....
....
....
....
....
....
....

*True to Your word, You let me catch my breath
and send me in the right direction.*
PSALM 23:3 THE MESSAGE

THOUGHT FOR THE DAY

There is always time for a nap.

Suzy Becker

HIGHLIGHT OF THE DAY

$\mathscr{M}$y soul finds rest in God alone; my salvation comes from Him.

PSALM 62:1 NIV

THOUGHT FOR THE DAY

You'll learn more about a road by traveling it than by consulting
all the maps in the world.

HIGHLIGHT OF THE DAY

Show me the right path, O Lord;
point out the road for me to follow.

PSALM 25:4 NLT

An adventure is only an inconvenience rightly considered. An inconvenience
is only an adventure wrongly considered.

G. K. Chesterton

HIGHLIGHT OF THE DAY

At the end of the journey we'll surely rest with God.
So let's keep at it and eventually arrive at the place of rest.
HEBREWS 4:9-10 THE MESSAGE

THOUGHT FOR THE DAY

Life is not a journey to the grave with the intention of arriving safely in
one pretty and well preserved piece, but to skid across the line broadside,
thoroughly used up, worn out, leaking oil, shouting GERONIMO!

Bill McKenna

HIGHLIGHT OF THE DAY

·····

*D*o you not know that in a race all the runners run, but only
one gets the prize? Run in such a way as to get the prize.
1 CORINTHIANS 9:24 NIV

THOUGHT FOR THE DAY

Go forth seeking adventure. Open your eyes, your ears, your mind, your heart,
your spirit and you'll find adventure everywhere.

Wilferd A. Peterson

Open your mouth and taste, open your eyes and see—
how good God is. Blessed are you who run to Him.

PSALM 34:8 THE MESSAGE

THOUGHT FOR THE DAY

Most new discoveries are suddenly-seen things that were always there.

Susanne K. Langer

HIGHLIGHT OF THE DAY

*G*ive thanks to the Lord, for He is good; for His lovingkindness is
everlasting. Who can speak of the mighty deeds of the Lord,
or can show forth all His praise?

PSALM 106:1-2 NASB

Happiness is not a station you arrive at, but a manner of traveling.

Margaret Lee Runbeck

The Lord your God will bless you in all your produce and in all
the work of your hands, so that you will be altogether joyful.

DEUTERONOMY 16:15 NASB

THOUGHT FOR THE DAY

A good friend is a connection to life—a tie to the past, a road to the future, the key to sanity in a totally insane world.

Lois Wyse

HIGHLIGHT OF THE DAY

There is a friend who sticks closer than a brother.
PROVERBS 18:24 NKJV

THOUGHT FOR THE DAY

Each of us may be sure that if God sends us on stony paths
He will provide us with strong shoes.

Alexander Maclaren

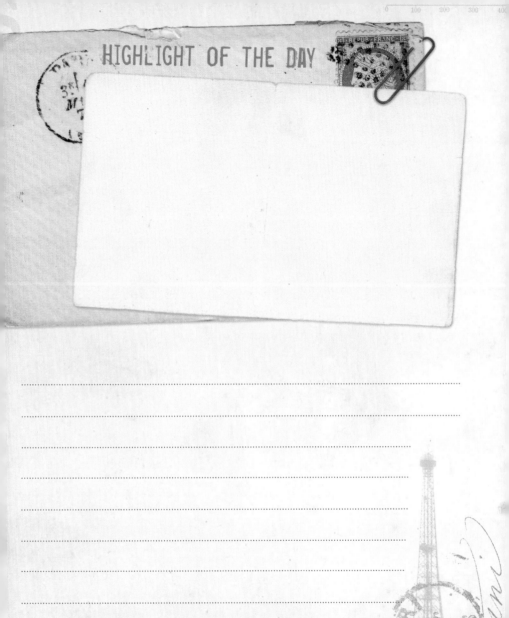

You will show me the path of life; in Your presence is fullness
of joy; at Your right hand are pleasures forevermore.

PSALM 16:11 NKJV

THOUGHT FOR THE DAY

Life begins each morning.... Each morning is the open door to a new world—
new vistas, new aims, new tryings.

Leigh Mitchell Hodges

HIGHLIGHT OF THE DAY

The faithful love of the Lord never ends! His mercies never cease.
Great is His faithfulness; His mercies begin afresh each morning.

LAMENTATIONS 3:22-23 NLT

THOUGHT FOR THE DAY

Meeting someone for the first time is like going on a treasure hunt.
What wonderful worlds we can find in others!

Edward E. Ford

HIGHLIGHT OF THE DAY

I have not stopped giving thanks to God for you.
I always remember you in my prayers.

EPHESIANS 1:16 NCV

THOUGHT FOR THE DAY

As we travel on life's way, we meet with angels everyday.

HIGHLIGHT OF THE DAY

_Do not neglect to show hospitality to strangers, for by this
some have entertained angels without knowing it._

HEBREWS 13:2 NASB

THOUGHT FOR THE DAY

Anything, everything, little or big becomes an adventure
when the right person shares it.

Kathleen Norris

HIGHLIGHT OF THE DAY

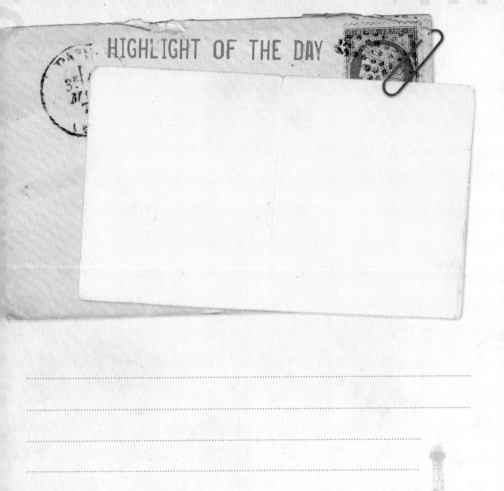

Share each other's burdens, and in this way
obey the law of Christ.

GALATIANS 6:2 NLT

THOUGHT FOR THE DAY

God invites you to vacation in His splendor. He invites you to feel the touch of
His hand. He invites you to feast at His table. He wants to spend time with you.

Max Lucado

The glory of God—let it last forever!
Let God enjoy His creation!
PSALM 104:31 THE MESSAGE

THOUGHT FOR THE DAY

I would like to travel light on this journey of life, to get rid of the encumbrances
I acquire each day.... I come to be only as I lose myself.

Madeleine L'Engle

*A*ll stride freely through wide open spaces as
I look for Your truth and Your wisdom.

PSALM 119:45 THE MESSAGE

THOUGHT FOR THE DAY

All I have seen teaches me to trust the Creator for all I have not seen.

Ralph Waldo Emerson

24,349

*Faith is the substance of things hoped for,
the evidence of things not seen.*
HEBREWS 11:1 NKJV

THOUGHT FOR THE DAY

The use of traveling is to regulate imagination by reality, and instead of
thinking how things may be, to see them as they are.

Samuel Johnson

HIGHLIGHT OF THE DAY

....

....

....

....

....

....

....

....

*Blessed are those who have not seen
and yet have believed.*
JOHN 20:29 NIV

THOUGHT FOR THE DAY

Rest is not idleness, and to lie sometimes on the grass under the trees on a summer's day, listening to the murmur of water...is by no means a waste of time.

Sir John Lubbock

HIGHLIGHT OF THE DAY

The Lord is my shepherd; I shall not want. He makes me to lie down in green pastures; He leads me beside the still waters.

PSALM 23:1-2 NKJV

THOUGHT FOR THE DAY

I found loveliness today down along life's broad highway....
Golden glow at break of day, joy in children at their play,
Scented odor of wild rose; peace I found where violet grows.

Carleton Everett Knox

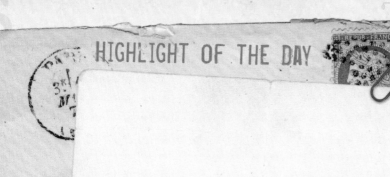

HIGHLIGHT OF THE DAY

....

....

....

....

....

....

....

....

Go in peace. The presence of the Lord
be with you on your way.

JUDGES 18:6 NKJV

THOUGHT FOR THE DAY

Isn't it splendid to think of all the things there are to find out about?
It just makes me feel glad to be alive—it's such an interesting world.

Lucy Maud Montgomery

24,349

God is wise in heart and mighty in strength.... He does great
things past finding out, yes, wonders without number.

JOB 9:4, 10 NKJV

THOUGHT FOR THE DAY

God has promised strength for the day, rest for the labor, light for the way,
grace for the trials, help from above, unfailing sympathy, undying love.

Annie Johnson Flint

HIGHLIGHT OF THE DAY

Then I will lead the blind along a way they never knew....
I will make the darkness become light for them,
and the rough ground smooth.

ISAIAH 42:16 NCV

*G*od alone knows the way to wisdom, He knows the
exact place to find it. He knows where everything
is on earth, He sees everything under heaven.

JOB 28:23 THE MESSAGE

It is God to whom and with whom we travel, and while He is the end
of our journey, He is also at every stopping place.

Elisabeth Elliot

HIGHLIGHT OF THE DAY

The Lord, before whom I have walked, will send His
angel with you to make your journey successful.
GENESIS 24:40 NASB

THOUGHT FOR THE DAY

The journey of a thousand miles starts with a single step.

Chinese Proverb

HIGHLIGHT OF THE DAY

Listen, my son, and be wise, and keep
your heart on the right path.
PROVERBS 23:19 NIV

THOUGHT FOR THE DAY

We are not alone on our journey. The God of love...sent us His only Son to be with us at all times and in all places, so that we never have to feel lost.

Henri J. M. Nouwen

HIGHLIGHT OF THE DAY

*G*od loved the world so much that He gave His one
and only Son so that whoever believes in Him
may not be lost, but have eternal life.

JOHN 3:16 NCV

THOUGHT FOR THE DAY

To know someone here or there with whom you feel there is an understanding in spite of distances or thoughts unexpressed—that can make of this earth a garden.

Goethe

HIGHLIGHT OF THE DAY

*A*ll sunshine and sovereign is God,
generous in gifts and glory.
PSALM 84:10 THE MESSAGE

THOUGHT FOR THE DAY

For the pathway that lies before me, my Heavenly Father knows—
I'll trust Him to unfold the moments just as He unfolds the rose.

My foot has held fast to His path; I have kept
His way and not turned aside.

JOB 23:11 NASB

THOUGHT FOR THE DAY

True contentment is a real, even an active, virtue—not only affirmative but creative. It is the power of getting out of any situation all there is in it.

G. K. Chesterton

....

....

....

....

....

....

....

....

....

....

....

....

....

....

....

....

....

....

HIGHLIGHT OF THE DAY

I know what it is to be in need, and I know what it is to have plenty. I have learned the secret of being content.

PHILIPPIANS 4:11-12 NIV

THOUGHT FOR THE DAY

Life is short and we never have enough time for gladdening the hearts of those who travel the way with us. O, be swift to love! Make haste to be kind.

Henri Frédéric Amiel

HIGHLIGHT OF THE DAY

The Lord has told you what is good, and this is what
He requires of you: to do what is right, to love mercy,
and to walk humbly with your God.

MICAH 6:8 NLT

We may run, walk, stumble, drive, or fly, but let us never lose sight of the reason for the journey, or miss a chance to see a rainbow on the way.

Gloria Gaither

HIGHLIGHT OF THE DAY

My child, don't lose sight of common sense and discernment.
Hang on to them, for they will refresh your soul.
They are like jewels on a necklace.

PROVERBS 3:21-22 NLT

THOUGHT FOR THE DAY

Our road will be smooth and untroubled no matter what care life may send;
if we travel the pathway together, and walk side by side with a friend.

Henry Van Dyke

HIGHLIGHT OF THE DAY

*M*ake every effort to keep yourselves united in the Spirit,
binding yourselves together with peace.

EPHESIANS 4:3 NLT

THOUGHT FOR THE DAY

Though I have seen the oceans and mountains, though I have read great books and seen great works of art,...there is nothing greater or more beautiful than those people I love.

Christopher de Vinck

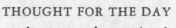

HIGHLIGHT OF THE DAY

May the Lord make your love for one another and for all people grow and overflow, just as our love for you overflows.

1 THESSALONIANS 3:12 NLT

THOUGHT FOR THE DAY

The gift of life unwraps itself through time; all we need to do
is sit back and enjoy its contents.

HIGHLIGHT OF THE DAY

*Shout and sing for joy, you people of Jerusalem, because the
Holy One of Israel does great things before your eyes.*

ISAIAH 12:6 NCV

THOUGHT FOR THE DAY

God puts each fresh morning, each new chance of life,
into our hands as a gift to see what we will do with it.

HIGHLIGHT OF THE DAY

May God give you more and more grace and peace as you
grow in your knowledge of God and Jesus our Lord.

2 PETER 1:2 NLT

THOUGHT FOR THE DAY

Life is what we are alive to. It is not length but breadth.... Be alive to...goodness, kindness, purity, love, history, poetry, music, flowers, stars, God, and eternal hope.

Maltbie D. Babcock

May our Lord Jesus Christ Himself and God our Father, who loved us and by His grace gave us eternal encouragement and good hope, encourage your hearts and strengthen you in every good deed and word.

2 THESSALONIANS 2:16-17 NIV

THOUGHT FOR THE DAY

When you're traveling, you are what you are right there and then. People don't have your past to hold against you. No yesterdays on the road.

William Least Heat Moon

HIGHLIGHT OF THE DAY

We grow like a flower in the field. After the wind blows,
the flower is gone, and there is no sign of where it was.
But the Lord's love...continues forever and ever.

PSALM 103:15-17 NCV

THOUGHT FOR THE DAY

For all of us, whether we walk old paths or blaze new trails,
friends remain important.

Lois Wyse

HIGHLIGHT OF THE DAY

*Two are better than one, because they have a good return for
their work: If one falls down, his friend can help him up.*

ECCLESIASTES 4:9-10 NIV

THOUGHT FOR THE DAY

No one realizes how beautiful it is to travel until he comes home
and rests his head on his old, familiar pillow.

Lin Yutang

HIGHLIGHT OF THE DAY

*C*ome to Me, all of you who are tired and have
heavy loads, and I will give you rest.
MATTHEW 11:28 NIV

Joys come from simple and natural things: mists over meadows,
sunlight on leaves, the path of the moon over water.

Sigurd F. Olson

HIGHLIGHT OF THE DAY

The heavens declare the glory of God, and the skies
announce what His hands have made.

<small>PSALM 19:1 NCV</small>

THOUGHT FOR THE DAY

There will always be the unknown. There will always be the unprovable.
But faith confronts those frontiers with a thrilling leap.
Then life becomes vibrant with adventure!

Robert Schuller

24,349

HIGHLIGHT OF THE DAY

By faith we understand that the entire universe was
formed at God's command, that what we now see did
not come from anything that can be seen.

HEBREWS 11:8-10 NLT

THOUGHT FOR THE DAY

May your footsteps set you upon a lifetime journey of love. May you wake each day with His blessings and sleep each night in His keeping. And may you always walk in His tender care.

*S*tand at the crossroads and look...ask where the good way is,
and walk in it, and you will find rest for your souls.

JEREMIAH 6:16 NIV

THOUGHT FOR THE DAY

Every day is an opportunity to make a new happy ending.
May you live all the days of your life.

Jonathan Swift